EXPLORING OUR
UNIVERSE

SPACE EXPLORATION

KELLY DOUDNA

Checkerboard
Library

An Imprint of Abdo Publishing
abdopublishing.com

abdopublishing.com

Published by Abdo Publishing, a division of ABDO, PO Box 398166, Minneapolis, Minnesota 55439. Copyright ©2017 by Abdo Consulting Group, Inc. International copyrights reserved in all countries. No part of this book may be reproduced in any form without written permission from the publisher. Checkerboard Library™ is a trademark and logo of Abdo Publishing.
Printed in the United States of America, North Mankato, Minnesota
102016
012017

THIS BOOK CONTAINS RECYCLED MATERIALS

Design: Emily O'Malley, Mighty Media, Inc.
Production: Mighty Media, Inc.
Editor: Paige Polinsky
Cover Photograph: NASA
Interior Photographs: Mighty Media, Inc. pp. 7, 19; NASA, pp. 11, 12, 13, 17, 21, 22, 23, 25, 26, 27; Shutterstock, pp. 5, 9, 10, 29; Wikimedia Commons, p. 15 (top and bottom)

Publisher's Cataloging-in-Publication Data

Names: Doudna, Kelly, author.
Title: Space exploration / by Kelly Doudna.
Description: Minneapolis, MN : Abdo Publishing, 2017. | Series: Exploring our universe | Includes bibliographical references and index.
Identifiers: LCCN 2016944828 | ISBN 9781680784077 (lib. bdg.) | ISBN 9781680797602 (ebook)
Subjects: LCSH: Astronautics--Juvenile literature. | Outer space--Exploration-- Juvenile literature.
Classification: DDC 629.4--dc23
LC record available at http://lccn.loc.gov/2016944828

CONTENTS

MISSION
EXPLORING SPACE

Have you ever wondered what's in space? Maybe you'd like to become an astronomer. You can get started in your own backyard. Track the path of the sun across the sky. Notice how the moon changes from one night to the next.

Looking Near

For centuries, we have studied space from the ground. In 1609, Galileo Galilei used a handheld telescope. Today, astronomers use huge mountaintop telescopes.

Looking Far

We can also explore space directly. The National Aeronautics and Space Administration (**NASA**) first landed humans on the moon during the Apollo missions. Today, astronauts study on the International Space Station (ISS).

On a clear night with little light pollution, you can see about 2,000 stars. With a telescope, you can spot even more!

Reaching for the Stars

Astronomers collect data from the farthest stretches of the universe. They can't observe everything directly. But they can use math and **physics** to make guesses. These guesses can teach us about our universe's past and future.

CHAPTER 1

WAVES AND LENSES

There are many types of telescopes. Some work from Earth. Others function in space. Different telescopes see different **light waves** of the electromagnetic spectrum.

The electromagnetic spectrum contains every type of light wave. This includes radio, microwave, **infrared**, and other invisible light waves. Special telescopes reveal these waves. They allow researchers to see more of the universe.

Telescopes on the ground must fight against Earth's atmosphere. Air turbulence warps the incoming data. Because of this, **observatories** are often located at high altitudes. The air at these heights contains fewer molecules. Fewer molecules means less turbulence.

Moisture also affects telescopes. Damp air can warp lenses. This is why many telescopes are in the desert. Desert air contains fewer water molecules.

THE ELECTROMAGNETIC SPECTRUM

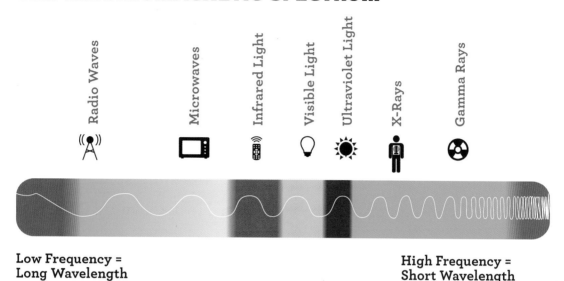

Low Frequency =
Long Wavelength

High Frequency =
Short Wavelength

Low-frequency waves, like radio waves, have longer wavelengths. High-frequency waves, like gamma rays, have shorter wavelengths. Instruments exist to detect every type of wave.

Space telescopes orbit Earth and the sun. There, they are beyond most atmospheric interference. They can detect fainter **wavelengths**. Astronomers combine images from multiple **light waves**. This gives them a more complete picture of what they observe.

CHAPTER 2

EARTH TELESCOPES

Telescopes reveal much about our galaxy. In 1609, Galileo became the first person to study space with a telescope. His telescope was small and simple. But he saw the moon's mountains and craters. He discovered Jupiter's four largest moons. And he even observed our solar system's home galaxy, the Milky Way.

Galileo's telescope was a refracting telescope. In a refracting telescope, light passes through glass lenses to the observer's eye. There are also reflecting telescopes. These use mirrors instead of glass lenses. The light bounces off the mirrors and into the observer's eye.

Reflecting telescopes eventually became much more popular than refracting telescopes. This is because mirrors are easier to make than glass lenses. Making telescopes with big, powerful mirrors was less expensive.

The first telescopes could only magnify objects on Earth. Galileo improved
existing telescope designs with a telescope that could peer into space.

Today's telescopes are more powerful than anything Galileo used. And they are stationed all over the world. Mauna Kea is a **dormant** volcano in Hawaii. Its summit is 13,796 feet (4,205 m) above sea level. The altitude and dry air make it a good telescope location.

The Keck and Keck II telescopes sit on Mauna Kea. Each has a mirror that is 33 feet (10 m) wide. The telescopes detect visible and **infrared** light. Scientists use them to measure the light of distant stars. By tracking changes, scientists found **exoplanets** orbiting these stars.

The Very Large Array (VLA) is in the New Mexico desert. It consists of 27 sensitive telescope dishes. They detect radio waves from space. Astronomers use them to study our **galaxy**'s center.

Keck and Keck II
telescopes

A dish is moved to prepare the VLA in September 1980. The telescope began operating in October of that year.

CHAPTER 3

SPACE TELESCOPES

The Hubble Space Telescope (HST) orbits 343 miles (552 km) above Earth. It studies four different **light waves**. In 2016, HST helped discover the oldest known **galaxy**, GN-z11. GN-z11 is about 13.4 billion years old. At its birth, the universe was only 400 million years old.

The Chandra X-ray **Observatory** is another space telescope. It observes the black hole at our galaxy's center. Black holes are dense objects formed by dying stars. Their extreme gravity sucks up nearby gases and stars.

The James Webb Space Telescope is under construction. In 2018, it will travel beyond Earth's orbit.

Hubble Space Telescope

The Chandra X-ray Observatory orbits
86,500 miles (139,000 km) above Earth.

There, it will study **infrared** waves. The James Webb
Space Telescope will see the oldest parts of our universe.
It will teach astronomers about the birth of our universe,
called the big bang. They will study young **galaxies**. They
will also search for **exoplanets** which could support life.

CHAPTER 4

NASA

HST and Chandra were both created by **NASA**. US President Dwight D. Eisenhower founded NASA in 1958 to advance space exploration. NASA was also a response to the Soviet Union's space program. The successful launch of the Soviet *Sputnik 1* **satellite** increased American scientists' desire to compete. What was known as the space race was born.

German engineer Wernher von Braun led America's rocket development. In the 1960s, his rockets sent the first American astronauts into orbit. Since then, NASA has led many different missions.

DID YOU KNOW ?

In 1951, a monkey named Yorick became the first monkey to survive a space flight. In 1957, Laika the dog became the first creature to orbit Earth.

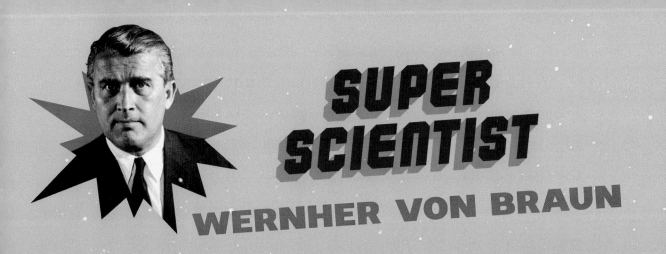

SUPER SCIENTIST
WERNHER VON BRAUN

German-born Wernher von Braun was a rocket scientist. During World War II, he developed the V-2 rocket for the German Nazi government. The German government used the V-2 to fire missiles at its enemies, the Allies. But von Braun didn't like this use of the rocket. In 1945, he surrendered to one of the Allies, the United States.

Von Braun began developing rockets for NASA. His Redstone rocket launched the first American satellite in 1958. Three years later, it took the first astronauts to space.

Von Braun was a brilliant engineer. He went on to make important contributions to space exploration.

A Redstone rocket carrying a chimpanzee named Ham launched in 1961.

In the United States, human spaceflight began with Project Mercury. The program involved six **manned** flights from 1961 to 1963. In 1961, Alan Shepard became the first American astronaut to leave Earth. The next year, John Glenn became the first to orbit Earth. These missions taught **NASA** about launching and recovering spacecraft.

Project Gemini was the next step in human spaceflight. It involved ten manned missions to space. In 1965, Ed White went on the first **spacewalk** from the Gemini IV **capsule**. Later that year, the Gemini VII capsule stayed in orbit for 14 days. It was a record at the time. Other Gemini capsules docked with each other while in orbit.

Meanwhile, NASA's Apollo program focused on lunar exploration. On July 20, 1969, the Apollo 11 spacecraft *Eagle* landed on the moon. Astronauts Neil Armstrong and Edwin "Buzz" Aldrin were aboard. Armstrong made history as the first man to walk on the moon.

The Apollo 11 astronauts spent 21 hours and 36 minutes on the moon's surface.

CHAPTER 5

SPACE SHUTTLES

In 1981, **NASA** started the Space Shuttle program. The program consisted of six shuttles. These shuttles launched and retrieved **satellites**. They also brought astronauts and supplies to and from the ISS.

In 1981, *Columbia* became the first shuttle to enter orbit. Two years later, the shuttle *Challenger* carried astronaut Sally Ride into orbit. She was the first American woman in space.

Discovery flew more missions than any other shuttle. It launched the world's most powerful telescope, the HST. Later, crews of the *Endeavor* and *Atlantis* shuttles repaired the HST.

DID YOU KNOW ?

Space shuttle missions could be very dangerous. In 1986, *Challenger* exploded during liftoff. *Columbia* broke apart on re-entry in 2003.

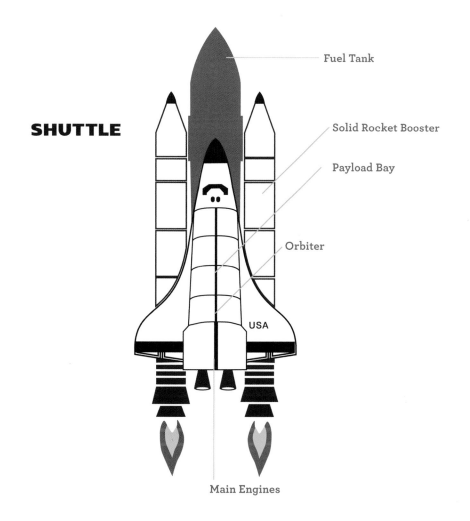

SHUTTLE

Fuel Tank

Solid Rocket Booster

Payload Bay

Orbiter

USA

Main Engines

The Space Shuttle program was successful. But it was also expensive and risky. Two shuttles were destroyed in accidents. Their crews did not survive. In 2011, the program ended.

CHAPTER 6

SPACE STATIONS

Space stations are vital to space exploration. Many experiments are conducted onboard them. The astronauts themselves are even studied! The knowledge gained is used to plan human missions to Mars and beyond.

SKYLAB

Skylab was the first US space station. It orbited Earth from 1973 to 1979. Skylab's astronauts learned how to work in space. They observed comets and **solar radiation**. They also studied the effects of low gravity on humans.

MIR

Space station *Mir* was operated by the Soviet Union, and later Russia. It was in orbit from 1986 to 2001. *Mir* could support three people at a time. It was made up of seven **modules** that fit together.

The US space shuttle *Atlantis* (*bottom*) docked at *Mir* in 1995.

The Shuttle-*Mir* Program ran from 1994 to 1997. **NASA** shuttles transported Russian and US astronauts, supplies, and equipment between Earth and *Mir*.

Sergei K. Krikalev (*left*), William M. Shepherd (*center*), and Yuri P. Gidzenko (*right*) made up the first crew to occupy the ISS.

INTERNATIONAL SPACE STATION

Space agencies from Europe, Canada, Russia, Japan, and the United States built the ISS in 1998. The station contains three laboratories. The largest is Japanese Experimental **Module** *Kibo*. Biology experiments are conducted there. The European Space Agency's Columbus lab studies **physics**.

The ISS crew consists of six astronauts from several different countries. They conduct experiments and observations. The ISS plans to remain in use through at least 2024.

TOOLS OF DISCOVERY

TWINS STUDY

The Twins Study ran from 2015 to 2016. During this time, NASA studied identical twin astronauts Scott and Mark Kelly. Scott spent 340 weightless days aboard the ISS. This is the longest continuous stay on the ISS to date. Mark stayed on Earth.

Identical twins are exact genetic copies of each other. Scientists ran the same tests on each twin. They studied the difference between the twins' results. This showed them the effects of living in zero gravity in space. This data will help scientists find ways in which to safely send humans to Mars.

Scientists compared Mark (*right*) and Scott's health, sleep patterns, and more during Scott's time on the ISS.

CHAPTER 7

SPACE PROBES

Space probes include orbiters, **landers,** and **rovers.**
Probes travel to planets, moons, asteroids, and comets
in our solar system. They also explore deep space. This
exploration leads to important discoveries!

PLANETARY PROBES

We are not yet able to send humans to Mars. It is too
far away. But in 2012, **NASA**'s Mars Science Laboratory
landed the *Curiosity* rover on Mars. *Curiosity* searched
for evidence of life. It also collected data important for
planning future human missions to Mars.

The orbiter Cassini-Huygens left Earth for Saturn
in 1997. It passed and studied Jupiter on the way. After
seven years, Cassini arrived at Saturn. Cassini explored
Saturn, its rings, and its moons. It taught scientists more

Technicians prepare a heat shield for the Mars Science Laboratory. It is the largest heat shield ever built for a planetary mission.

about gaseous planet systems. Cassini carried the Huygens **lander**. Huygens landed on Saturn's moon Titan. It was the first lander in the outer solar system.

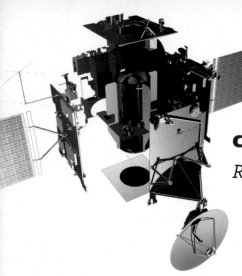

COMET CAPERS

Rosetta was the first spacecraft to orbit a
comet. It mapped the irregular shape of
Comet 67P. It also studied the gases in
the comet's tail. *Rosetta* had a **lander**,
called *Philae*. *Philae* explored 67P's surface.
There, it collected dust and gas samples.

Philae detected organic matter on the comet. Organic
compounds are the building blocks of life. Some scientists
believe that by crashing to Earth, early comets brought
these compounds with them. These were the seeds for life
on Earth.

SOLAR SYSTEM ESCAPEES

Spacecraft *Voyager 1* and *Voyager 2* were launched in 1977.
They explored Jupiter, Saturn, Uranus, and Neptune. They
were then reprogrammed to fly beyond our solar system.
This is called the interstellar zone.

An illustration of NASA's *Voyager 1*. In 1998, *Voyager 1* became the most distant human-made object in space.

It took *Voyager 1* more than 40 years to reach the interstellar zone! *Voyager 2* followed in 2016. Both probes send information back to Earth. They have traveled farther than any spacecraft before them. And the farther they go, the more we will learn about the universe we call home.

EXPLORATION GUIDEBOOK

Famous Firsts

- Astronomer to use a telescope: Galileo Galilei (1609)
- Rocket launch: V-2 (1942)
- Human to orbit Earth: Yuri Gagarin (1961)
- Mission to fly to another planet: Mariner 2 to Venus (1962)
- Manned lunar landing: Apollo 11 mission (1969)
- Human to walk on the moon: Neil Armstrong (1969)
- Detected black hole: Cygnus X-1, discovered by Charles Thomas Bolton, Louise Webster, and Paul Murdin (1971)

DID YOU KNOW ?

In 1983, Pioneer 10 became the first space probe to leave the solar system. It carried a gold plaque that showed information about human beings and our solar system.

- Telescope in orbit: **Infrared Astronomical Satellite** (1983)
- Permanent space telescope: Hubble Space Telescope (1990)
- Mission to leave the solar system: *Voyager 1* (2013)
- Mission to orbit another planet: Mariner 9 around Mars (1971)
- **Manned** mission to another planet: Unknown. Scientists believe it could be possible by 2025 or 2030

The VLA radio telescope in New Mexico

GLOSSARY

allies — people, groups, or nations united for some special purpose. During World War II Great Britain, France, the United States, and the Soviet Union were called the Allies.

capsule — the part of a spacecraft in which the crew travels.

dormant — not active but able to become active.

exoplanet — a planet that exists outside of our solar system.

galaxy — a very large group of stars and planets.

infrared — energy transmitted by waves, which can be felt as heat.

lander — a space vehicle designed to land on a celestial body.

light wave — an amount of light energy that travels through air or water in the shape of a wave.

manned — carrying or done by a person.

module — a self-contained, independent part of a spacecraft having a specific function.

NASA — National Aeronautics and Space Administration. NASA is a US government agency that manages the nation's space program and conducts flight research.

Nazi — the political party that controlled Germany under Adolf Hitler from 1933 to 1945.

observatory — a place or a building for observing the weather or the stars.

physics — a science that studies matter and energy and how they interact.

rover — a vehicle used for exploring the surface of space objects.

satellite — an object, either natural or manufactured, that orbits a larger heavenly body. A manufactured satellite relays scientific information back to Earth.

solar radiation — a type of energy given off by the sun.

spacewalk — an activity in which an astronaut does work outside a spacecraft while it is in space.

twin — one of two children born at the same birth to the same mother.

wavelength — the distance between one point on a light wave and the next.

World War II — from 1939 to 1945, fought in Europe, Asia, and Africa. Great Britain, France, the United States, the Soviet Union, and their allies were on one side. Germany, Italy, Japan, and their allies were on the other side.

WEBSITES

To learn more about Exploring Our Universe, visit booklinks.abdopublishing.com. These links are routinely monitored and updated to provide the most current information available.

INDEX